NATIONAL
GEOGRAPHIC

AMERICAN DOCUMENTS

The Bill of Rights

Judith Lloyd Yero

Picture Credits

Cover (flag) Photodisc/Getty Images; cover (document), 7 courtesy Library of Congress; cover (foreground) Joseph Sohm/ChromoSohm Inc/Corbis; p. 1 Courtesy of JPFO.org; pp. 2-3, 14 Flip Schulke/Corbis; p. 4 AFP/Corbis; pp. 4-5 Todd A. Gipstein/Corbis; pp. 6, 13, 17, 22, 24 AP Wide World Photos; pp. 8, 16, 19, 26 Bettmann/Corbis; pp. 9-11, 25 (top) Corbis; pp. 12 (top), 13 (bottom) Hulton Archive/Getty Images; p. 12 (bottom) Historical Society of the Court of New York; pp. 15, 25 (bottom), 29 David Butow/Corbis SABA; p. 18 Leif Skoogfors/Corbis; p. 20 PhotoEdit Inc.; p. 21 Royalty-Free/Corbis; p. 23 Mark Peterson/Corbis; p. 27 Reuters New Media/Corbis; p. 28 Wally McNamee/Corbis; p. 30 Michael Yamashita/Corbis; p. 31 Swim Ink/Corbis. Printed by permission of the Norman Rockwell Family Agency. © 1943 The Norman Rockwell Family Entities.

Produced through the worldwide resources of the National Geographic Society, John M. Fahey, Jr., President and Chief Executive Officer; Gilbert M. Grosvenor, Chairman of the Board; Nina D. Hoffman, Executive Vice President and President, Books and Education Publishing Group.

Prepared by National Geographic School Publishing and Children s Books

Ericka Markman, Senior Vice President and President, Children's Books and Education Publishing Group; Steve Mico, Vice President, Editorial Director; Marianne Hiland, Executive Editor; Anita Schwartz, Project Editor, Suzanne Patrick Fonda, Children's Books Project Editor; Jim Hiscott, Design Manager; Kristin Hanneman, Illustrations Manager; Diana Bourdrez, Picture Editor; Matt Wascavage, Manager of Publishing Services; Sean Philpotts, Production Manager.

Manufacturing and Quality Management

Christopher A. Liedel, Chief Financial Officer; Phillip L. Schlosser, Director; Clifton M. Brown, Manager.

Consultants/Reviewers

Dr. Paul Finkelman, Chapman Distinguished Professor of Law, University of Tulsa Law School, Tulsa, Oklahoma

Dr. Margit E. McGuire, School of Education, Seattle University, Seattle, Washington

Book Development

Nieman Inc.

Book Design

Steven Curtis Design, Inc.

Art Direction

Dan Banks, Project Design Company

Photo Research

Corrine L. Brock, In the Lupe, Inc.

Copyright © 2006 National Geographic Society. All Rights Reserved. Reproduction in whole or in part of the contents without written permission from the publisher is prohibited.

ISBN 0-7922-5395-7 (hardcover)

ISBN 0-7922-5396-5 (library binding)

Previously published as *Documents of Freedom: The Bill of Rights* (National Geographic Reading Expeditions). Copyright © 2004 ISBN 0-7922-4552-0 (paperback)

Published by the NATIONAL GEOGRAPHIC SOCIETY
1145 17th Street, N.W.
Washington, D.C. 20036-4688

Printed in the U.S.A.

Table of Contents

Introduction

Imagine what your life would be like if:

- You could be arrested for writing things government officials didn't like.
- The police could search you and take away your property—for no reason you could figure out.
- You could be tortured into making a confession and it would be enough evidence to send you to jail.

That is how it is in some countries in the world today. Before the American Revolution, some of those things happened here! It's not that way any more.

The U.S. Constitution is our plan for government. It was written in 1787 to give the states a national government strong enough for the new country to work.

Americans have the right to worship as they choose. Here, leaders of different religions pledge allegiance at an interfaith service.

At first, many people were against the Constitution. They said it made the government too big and too powerful. Many people thought it should have a bill of rights to protect individuals from government abuse. For the Constitution to go into effect, 9 of the 13 states had to **ratify**, or approve, it. Arguments raged on for nearly a year. Finally, by the summer of 1788, nine states had accepted it. For many people, their "yes" vote came only after they were promised the Constitution would have a bill of rights.

The **Bill of Rights** is the first ten **amendments**, or changes, to our Constitution. Why did people feel so strongly? What does the Bill of Rights say? Let's find out.

Americans have the right to protest peacefully.

EARTH DAY
1990
WASHINGTON
D.C.

On Display

In 1789, Congress sent the states 12 amendments to approve. By 1791, they had approved ten amendments, now known as the Bill of Rights. Each state got an official copy. Congress had its own copy, which is kept in the National Archives in Washington, D.C.

Who "Wrote" It?

The handwritten copy on display in the National Archives was probably written by William Lambert, an assistant clerk in the House of Representatives.

Who Signed It?

Only four people signed the Bill of Rights: Frederick Augustus Muhlenberg, Speaker of the House of Representatives; John Adams, Vice-President of the United States and President of the Senate; and the chief Senate and House clerks as witnesses.

Which States?

Eleven states ratified the Bill of Rights. Three—Georgia, Connecticut, and Massachusetts—did not. The first state to ratify it was New Jersey, on November 20, 1789. Virginia was the last, on December 15, 1791.

no person shall be... deprived of life, liberty, or property, without due process of law...

Visitors to the Supreme Court Building in Washington, D.C.

Congress of the United States,

begun and held at the City of New York, on

Wednesday the fourth of March, one thousand seven hundred and eightynine.

THE Conventions of a number of the States, having at the time of their adopting the Constitution, expressed a desire, in order to prevent misconstruction or abuse of its powers, that further declaratory and restrictive clauses should be added: And as extending the ground of public confidence in the Government, will best ensure the beneficent ends of its institution.

RESOLVED by the Senate and House of Representatives of the United States of America, in Congress assembled, two thirds of both Houses concurring, that the following Articles be proposed to the Legislatures of the several States, as amendments to the Constitution of the United States, all, or any of which Articles, when ratified by three fourths of the said Legislatures, to be valid to all intents and purposes, as part of the said Constitution; viz.

ARTICLES in addition to, and Amendment of the Constitution of the United States of America, proposed by Congress, and ratified by the Legislatures of the several States, pursuant to the fifth Article of the original Constitution.

Article the first... After the first enumeration required by the first Article of the Constitution, there shall be one Representative for every thirty thousand, until the number shall amount to one hundred, after which the proportion shall be so regulated by Congress, that there shall be not less than one hundred Representatives, nor less than one Representative for every forty thousand persons, until the number of Representatives shall amount to two hundred, after which the proportion shall be so regulated by Congress, that there shall not be less than two hundred Representatives, nor more than one Representative for every fifty thousand persons.

Article the second... No law, varying the compensation for the services of the Senators and Representatives, shall take effect, until an election of Representatives shall have intervened.

Article the third... Congress shall make no law respecting an establishment of religion, or prohibiting the free exercise thereof; or abridging the freedom of speech, or of the press; or the right of the people peaceably to assemble, and to petition the Government for a redress of grievances.

Article the fourth... A well regulated militia, being necessary to the security of a free State, the right of the people to keep and bear arms, shall not be infringed.

Article the fifth... No soldier shall, in time of peace be quartered in any house, without the consent of the owner, nor in time of war, but in a manner to be prescribed by law.

Article the sixth... The right of the people to be secure in their persons, houses, papers, and effects, against unreasonable searches and seizures, shall not be violated, and no Warrants shall issue, but upon probable cause, supported by oath or affirmation, and particularly describing the place to be searched, and the persons or things to be seized.

Article the seventh... No person shall be held to answer for a capital, or otherwise infamous crime, unless on a presentment or indictment of a Grand Jury, except in cases arising in the land or naval forces, or in the Militia, when in actual service in time of war or public danger; nor shall any person be subject for the same offence to be twice put in jeopardy of life or limb; nor shall be compelled in any criminal case to be a witness against himself, nor be deprived of life, liberty, or property, without due process of law; nor shall private property be taken for public use, without just compensation.

Article the eighth... In all criminal prosecutions, the accused shall enjoy the right to a speedy and public trial, by an impartial jury of the State and district wherein the crime shall have been committed, which district shall have been previously ascertained by law, and to be informed of the nature and cause of the accusation; to be confronted with the witnesses against him; to have compulsory process for obtaining witnesses in his favor, and to have the assistance of counsel for his defence.

Article the ninth... In suits at common law, where the value in controversy shall exceed twenty dollars, the right of trial by jury shall be preserved, and no fact tried by a jury, shall be otherwise re-examined in any Court of the United States, than according to the rules of the common law.

Article the tenth... Excessive bail shall not be required, nor excessive fines imposed, nor cruel and unusual punishments inflicted.

Article the eleventh... The enumeration in the Constitution, of certain rights, shall not be construed to deny or disparage others retained by the people.

Article the twelfth... The powers not delegated to the United States by the Constitution, nor prohibited by it to the States, are reserved to the States respectively, or to the people.

ATTEST,

Frederick Augustus Muhlenberg, Speaker of the House of Representatives.

John Adams, Vice President of the United States, and President of the Senate.

John Beckley, Clerk of the House of Representatives.
Sam. A. Otis Secretary of the Senate.

Five Freedoms

Religion, speech, the press, assembly, and petition—these freedoms are guaranteed in the First Amendment.

★

Freedom of Religion

At the time of the colonies, most countries had an official religion. People who belonged to other religions were often **persecuted,** or not treated fairly. The **Puritans** came to America to escape this persecution. Then they turned around and did the same thing.

Anne Hutchinson preaching in Massachusetts

One Puritan woman in the Massachusetts Bay Colony disagreed with the leaders. Anne Hutchinson held religious meetings in her home instead of the church. She told people that they could speak to God themselves. They didn't need ministers to do it for them. The leaders of the colony were furious. In 1637, they arrested Hutchinson, tried her, and threw her out of the colony.

Things were not so different 150 years later. People in Virginia were getting ready to approve the Constitution. There, the Church of England was the official religion. Baptists were persecuted. Some Baptist ministers had been publicly whipped and jailed for preaching. One, Reverend John Leland, told James Madison about it. Madison, the "father of the Constitution," was shocked. Now he understood why the Bill of Rights was needed. After the Constitution was ratified in 1788, he led Congress to add it.

It begins with freedom of religion. The First Amendment guarantees us two kinds of religious freedom:

- We are free from any official religion.
- We are free to practice any religion—or none at all.

What sorts of activities could make a religion "established"? Our courts decide. Can public school sporting events begin with a prayer? The courts say "no." Government buildings and government-run schools—that is, public schools—can't sponsor religious activities. If they did, they would be establishing religion.

"Congress shall make no law regarding the establishment of religion"

This is how the First Amendment begins. There is no "established," or official, religion in the United States. And Congress cannot "prohibit the free exercise" of religion.

James Madison

The main writer of the Constitution was a gracious, charming lawyer from Virginia. He had helped to write that state's constitution. He was also an author of *The Federalist*. This series of articles helped persuade Americans to vote for the Constitution.

A protest in 1939 by Americans opposed to U.S. involvement in World War II

Freedom of Speech

In a free society, people are able to talk about what is happening. They discuss issues and make their own decisions. They can criticize their leaders. They can share their ideas.

Free speech is important to everyday life. We often take it for granted. Imagine having ideas you could not share. In many places in the world, this is what happens.

Talking is not the only thing protected by free speech. The courts have ruled that speech includes art, music, activities—even clothing. You can wear t-shirts with slogans or sing songs about how you feel. These are ways to **express** opinions and ideas. The First Amendment protects freedom of expression.

The First Amendment protects only speech and expression that does not cause a "clear and present danger." You cannot encourage people to commit a crime or to riot. For example, yelling "fire" in a crowded building as a joke would be a crime.

When the Bill of Rights was written, people could communicate with one another only in person or by letter. Today, we have the Internet. This technology has raised new issues about freedom of expression. Some people spread messages from terrorists and hate groups. Some people use the Internet to make plans for unlawful activities. Lawmakers are concerned about these uses of the Internet. Can they pass laws to stop certain activities? They must be careful. Laws can prevent crimes, but they cannot stop free expression.

Ideas are powerful. Some people's ideas make other people angry. Jokes about people's race or nationality are cruel. Plays and paintings that mock heroes or religious leaders make some people furious. However, the First Amendment protects these expressions. Speech is not illegal just because it is cruel, unpopular, or upsetting. We have to put up with some bad ideas in order to be sure we get the good ones. This is part of being free.

Environmentalists exercising freedom of expression in 1987 at the Lincoln Memorial in Washington, D.C.

Freedom of the Press

The **press** are the people who make information available to others. In colonial times, the press largely produced newspapers. Colonial lawmakers sometimes tried to control the press when newspapers criticized public officials.

In the mid-1730s, colonist John Peter Zenger published many articles that criticized New York's royal governor. They were printed in his newspaper, the *New York Weekly*. The governor got fed up with Zenger and had him charged with unfairly damaging his reputation.

During Zenger's trial, his lawyer asked, how could telling the truth be a crime? The judge ordered the jury to find Zenger guilty, but the jury agreed with Zenger. They found him innocent.

Zenger's lawyer argued that the press had a right to print the truth.

Allowing reporters (such as the man lower right) to travel with U.S. military units during the 2003 Iraq war raised fears of government control of the news.

Today, in addition to newspapers, the press includes the people who produce magazines, radio, TV, and even Internet sites—all the **media**. Freedom of the press protects their right to express their opinions and ideas in writing. We are a democracy. We elect our leaders and our lawmakers. Writers must be free to publish what they find.

Freedom of the press has brought about great changes in this country. Thomas Paine published his pamphlet *Common Sense* just before the American Revolution. It convinced many colonists of the need to declare America's independence from Britain. Between October 1787 and May 1788, a series of essays called *The Federalist* appeared in several New York newspapers. These essays persuaded New Yorkers to approve the U.S. Constitution. In the early 1850s, a book called *Uncle Tom's Cabin* caused many Americans to oppose slavery. Between 1972 and 1974, a series of articles in the *Washington Post* reported on unlawful acts committed by President Richard Nixon and helped force him to resign.

Harriet Beecher Stowe

The author of *Uncle Tom's Cabin* wrote about a slave so full of love that he forgave the people who mistreated him. It was first published in a magazine, one chapter at a time. People could hardly wait to read the next part. When it appeared as a book in 1852, 300,000 copies were sold the first year! Stowe persuaded many people that slavery had to end.

Right to Assemble

The right to **assemble** is necessary to free speech. It allows people to get together to discuss ideas or to make their complaints known. That is, they have the right to protest.

Before the American Revolution, British troops broke up groups of people talking on the street. British governors banned town meetings. The British assumed that the colonists could not plan a revolt if they could not talk about it. The colonists who planned the Revolution had to meet in secret. When it came time to build a new government after the Revolution, people remembered the importance of the right of assembly.

The First Amendment guarantees that people can meet to talk about their ideas. They have the right to try to change the opinions of others through peaceful demonstrations. During the 1950s and 1960s, Dr. Martin Luther King, Jr., and others marched against racial **prejudice** and **discrimination**. Their actions got the government to pass laws that made racial discrimination illegal in many areas of American life.

Martin Luther King, Jr.
Hundreds of thousands of people gathered in Washington, D.C., to hear Dr. King give his famous "I Have a Dream" speech. In gathering together, they were showing support for a message that was changing America. They were making use of their right to assemble.

The right to assemble covers everything from marching in a Fourth of July parade, belonging to a political party, or joining an Internet chat group. You have a right to join groups, and the groups have a right to meet.

When people assemble, they are not allowed to block streets or to create traffic jams. They cannot march across private property. They cannot chain themselves in the doorway of a public building to keep people from entering. Carrying a picket sign is legal, but stopping workers from getting to their jobs is not.

People in Washington, D.C., come together to try to influence U.S. foreign policy.

In 1923, members of the League of Women Voters brought a mile-long petition to Washington, D.C.

Redress means "to set right." *Grievances* are the wrongs or complaints that the people have. When this phrase was written, people wanted to be certain they could ask the government to do the right thing for them without being punished.

Right to Petition

What happens when people don't like what their government does? How can they get the government to change? Before the Revolution, representatives of the colonies sent Britain's King George many respectful letters. These letters, or **petitions**, explained that the king's policies took away the colonists' rights. The petitions politely asked the king to fix their problems. The king ignored the colonists' petitions and called them traitors.

The First Amendment protects the right to ask our leaders to stop doing things we believe are wrong. We cannot be put in jail for making such suggestions.

The right to petition is also used to ask government for things. People might ask lawmakers to pass a law, change a law, or cancel a law. People have sent petitions to the government in Washington, D.C., asking for laws to protect air and water quality. People have petitioned their state government to lower their taxes. In some states, voters have asked their state lawmakers to ban the use of cell phones in cars. A town government might get petitions to put a stop sign at a dangerous corner. You might petition your city government to build a swimming pool.

A health-care worker helps a woman sign a petition to keep federal health-care funds for the elderly.

Protection

The colonists' homes, in British tradition, were safe, even from the king. The Second, Third, and Fourth Amendments extend this protection to American homes and communities.

★

Second Amendment

Do you remember when Paul Revere called the villagers and farmers out to fight? He rode out on horseback shouting, "The British are coming!" The minutemen who answered his call were a **militia**. They were armed to protect their communities.

Soldiers in a National Guard unit are a militia.

A militia is an army of part-time soldiers who are ready to protect their fellow citizens in time of emergencies. Each colony had a militia. These citizen-soldiers helped defend their communities. They helped to preserve law and order. Today, the state police and the National Guard do the work of the early militias.

The Second Amendment says the national government can not keep a state from having guns and other weapons. Many Americans believe that the "right to keep and bear arms" also gives every citizen the right to own guns.

People use guns to hunt and for target practice. Some people have gun collections. However, lawmakers have put limits on gun ownership to keep communities safe. In most cities, people have to get a permit to own a gun. Certain kinds of guns are not legal. People convicted of a crime can not own a gun. The courts have agreed these laws do not go against the Second Amendment.

"a well-regulated militia being necessary"

The Second Amendment begins with these words. The men who wrote the Bill of Rights gave this reason for the guarantee that "the right of the people to keep and bear arms shall not be infringed."

Third Amendment

This amendment says that, in peacetime, the government can not make people give housing to soldiers. Does that sound odd? Well, the British had forced some colonists to let British soldiers live in their homes. In some ways, the Third Amendment is the most successful. Congress has never tried to put soldiers in civilians' homes.

The Fourth Amendment

Many people say the Fourth Amendment protects "the right to privacy." That is because it says police or other government officials cannot search people or their homes unless there is a good reason to believe they have committed a crime. The government cannot snoop around in your business just in case you are doing something wrong.

Sometimes, the right to privacy is less important than other issues. Parents, teachers, and other school officials have the duty to protect children. They have the right to search children's rooms and lockers.

The men who wrote the Bill of Rights could not have imagined the kinds of searches possible today. Your "papers" include your telephone calls, e-mail files, and the history of Internet sites visited. There are records of the books you have checked out of libraries and the videos you have rented. There are your doctor's records about you. There are your school records. It is hard to do anything today that does not leave a record! The Fourth Amendment protects against any unreasonable government searches of your records.

The courts have given school officials the right to search students' lockers.

Since the September 11 terrorist attacks, airport security has been increased.

The Bill of Rights protects individual rights. There are times when the safety of a group is more important than the privacy of an individual. For example, the terrorist attack on September 11, 2001, caused many people to want the government to look hard for terrorists. People expect to be searched before getting on an airplane. Since the government can track Internet sites, should they investigate people who visit the ones that tell how to make bombs?

Questions like this end up in Congress and often in the courts. The answer is not as simple as it seems. People worry that giving up some rights can lead to losing many more rights. Remember, experience with a harsh government is the reason the Bill of Rights was written.

"unreasonable searches and seizures"

For a search to be "reasonable" there has to be "probable cause." There needs to be a good reason. A judge needs to agree that it is likely that evidence of a crime would probably be found in the search.

21

Rights of the Accused

Innocent until proven guilty—that idea is the cornerstone of our legal system. The Fifth, Sixth, and Seventh Amendments protect the rights of people accused of a crime.

★

Fifth Amendment

This amendment guarantees that the government has to go through proper steps to decide if a person is guilty and should be punished. Many rules exist now about what is and what is not allowed as evidence in a trial. They are meant to help the court find the truth.

Here is what the Fifth Amendment says:

- If the crime you are charged with carries a death penalty, a grand jury must agree there is enough evidence to hold a trial.

- If you have been found innocent of a crime, you cannot be tried for it again.

- You cannot be forced to **testify**, give evidence, against yourself. Have you ever heard of people "taking the fifth"? That means they are refusing to answer questions in court because the answers might make them appear guilty, even if they are really innocent.

- You cannot be punished, or "deprived of life, liberty, or property," without due process of law.

The Miranda Warning

In 1963, a man named Ernesto Miranda was arrested for kidnapping. When the police questioned him, Miranda admitted to the crime. Later in court, his lawyer argued that Miranda did not fully know his rights. Now, police read the "Miranda Warning" to every person they arrest. "You have the right to remain silent . . . ." The warning also says, "You have a right to have an attorney present during questioning." If a person cannot afford a lawyer, then the court will pay for one.

"No person shall be… deprived of life, liberty, or property without due process of law."

Due process refers to the "proper steps" set out in our laws for criminal matters. All the steps—arresting, questioning, accusing, holding a trial, and passing a sentence— are part of the process. In each of those steps, there are protections for an accused person.

Anyone arrested for a crime in the United States is given the Miranda Warning.

An accused person is tried by a jury of his peers.

Sixth Amendment

Imagine you have been arrested and thrown in jail. You do not know why. After months, you go to court. The "evidence" against you is all just rumors, and the judge has already decided you are guilty. You don't have a lawyer. You cannot ask any questions of the witnesses. This crime happened at the very time you were playing baseball. You cannot call your coach or teammates to come say where you were. What chance would you have?

The Sixth Amendment protects you from this happening. It guarantees that people charged with crimes will get:

- a speedy trial
- a public trial
- a jury of fair-minded people from the same state and area where the crime happened
- the knowledge of the charges against them
- the right to see who is testifying against them and have their lawyers question those people

"an impartial jury"

When a jury is being chosen, the judge and lawyers on both sides ask the people questions. They ask if they have heard about the case. They listen for things that might show a person has prejudices. They choose people who can ignore what they have read or heard and can make up their own minds.

It may not seem as if trials are speedy. It takes time for both sides to prepare their case. The police must search for evidence. Witnesses must be found. The lawyers need to do research into decisions in other trials that were similar. There are many cases for the court to hear. A trial might not take place for months or longer, even after everyone is ready.

Television did not exist when the Bill of Rights was written. Should trials be on TV? Some people say that television helps the public know what is going on. Others say that TV cameras turn a courtroom trial into a "three-ring circus." They say that lawyers and witnesses act dramatic and take too long because they are "on TV." State legislatures could decide this. If they do not, judges are the boss in their courtrooms. They can decide whether or not to allow TV cameras.

Americans are still debating whether trials should be televised.

Hugo Black

In 1963, the Supreme Court heard a case about a man named Clarence Gideon. He was too poor to get a lawyer for his criminal trial. The trial judge would not pay for one, and Gideon was found guilty. Justice Black wrote the Supreme Court's decision. He said it seemed "obvious" that you could not have a fair trial if you were not represented by a lawyer.

Dunking a person in a pond was an acceptable punishment for certain offenses in early America.

Seventh Amendment

Not all court cases are about crimes. Some cases seek to solve disagreements about property or money. The Seventh Amendment says that people in these **civil lawsuits** have a right to a jury trial if the amount is $20 or more. Back when this was written, $20 was equal to about 40 days of pay. Today, you would not ask for a jury trial over something worth only $20.

Eighth Amendment

The Eighth Amendment says that the punishment should fit the crime. Punishment cannot be "excessive." A judge cannot send a person to prison for life for ten parking tickets. A judge cannot fine someone $100,000 for not having a valid driver's license. Those punishments don't fit the crimes.

"excessive bail shall not be required"

Unless they are dangerous, people accused of crimes do not have to stay in jail until their trial. The court gives them the chance to post bail. That means they pay a sum of money that will be returned when they show up for the trial.

Punishments cannot be "cruel and unusual." The Bill of Rights does not let a judge invent bizarre punishments. Guilty criminals deserve to be punished. Society as a whole must agree that the punishment is normal and expected.

Today, many people believe that the death penalty is a cruel and unusual punishment. Almost all democracies have outlawed it. Only a few still use it. In the United States, people debate this point. If an innocent person is executed for a crime, there is not any way to fix it. You will certainly hear a lot more about this subject in your lifetime.

"cruel and unusual punishment"

Different societies have very different ideas about what is an acceptable punishment. In some countries, a person can have a hand cut off for stealing! In the United States, such a punishment would be seen as cruel and unusual.

Supporters of the death penalty hold a candlelight vigil for the victims of terrorist Timothy McVeigh on the day of his execution in 2001.

Limits to Power

The Bill of Rights protects individuals. It is a document that limits the power of the federal government. These last two amendments make that clear.

★

Ninth Amendment

Do people have any rights other than those in the Bill of Rights? The Ninth Amendment says "yes." Just because a right is not named does not mean it does not exist. It should "not be construed"—not be taken to mean—that other rights of individuals are not real or are not important.

The Ninth Amendment does not give the courts help in deciding what other rights people have. Judges have to use their training.

Although the rights of the disabled are not mentioned in the Bill of Rights, the Ninth Amendment protects them.

They look at how society is changing. Other amendments may help them decide. For example, the Fourth Amendment has encouraged courts to rule that people have the right to do what they want in private, as long as they do not harm anyone.

The courts have agreed we also have the right to:

- travel throughout America and outside the country
- get married
- raise and educate children as we want to

In addition the courts are clarifying the right to:

- an education
- a job
- housing

Tenth Amendment

The Tenth Amendment guarantees that the national government has only the powers that the Constitution gives it, and nothing more. This Amendment keeps the government and the people in balance. The United States government cannot take on more powers than it gets from the Constitution. All other powers belong either to the state governments or to the people.

The Ninth Amendment supports the right of Americans to travel freely,

The Test of Time

People insisted that the Constitution include a bill of rights to protect individual rights. Their love of freedom has become part of what we Americans call our heritage.

The Founders of our nation would be amazed at how life in the United States has changed. Yet, what is really amazing is that the Constitution and Bill of Rights grew and changed with the times. Millions of people have come to America to share in the life of freedom these documents helped create.

Every year, new citizens are sworn in as people come to the United States for the freedoms protected in our Bill of Rights.

Glossary

amendment a legally adopted change to a law or a body of laws

assemble to come together in a group

Bill of Rights the first ten amendments to the U.S. Constitution. A bill of rights is a formal statement of the rights and freedoms considered essential to a group of people.

civil lawsuit a court case about money or property, not about a crime

discrimination treating people unfairly and differently because they belong to a group, such as a race or a religion

express to make things known, to communicate in some way

media TV, radio, newspapers, magazines, and other mass communication

militia an army of citizens called out in time of emergency

persecute to harass or harm, especially because of religion, politics, or race

petition a formal written document asking for a right or a benefit from an authority, such as a government

prejudice hatred of a particular race, religion, or group

press the people who make information available to others through newspapers, magazines, TV, radio, or other public media

Puritans members of a religious group in Britain and in the British colonies who followed a strict moral code

ratify to approve and make official

testify to give facts or state the truth under oath in court

Norman Rockwell's famous World War II poster reminded Americans they were fighting to protect their freedoms.

The Bill of Rights

Amendments I - X
from The Constitution
of the United States

Ratified December 15, 1791

Amendment I

Congress shall make no law respecting an establishment of religion, or prohibiting the free exercise thereof; or abridging the freedom of speech, or of the press; or the right of the people peaceably to assemble, and to petition the Government for a redress of grievances.

Amendment II

A well regulated Militia, being necessary to the security of a free State, the right of the people to keep and bear Arms, shall not be infringed.

Amendment III

No Soldier shall, in time of peace be quartered in any house, without the consent of the Owner, nor in time of war, but in a manner to be prescribed by law.

Amendment IV

The right of the people to be secure in their persons, houses, papers, and effects, against unreasonable searches and seizures, shall not be violated, and no Warrants shall issue, but upon probable cause, supported by Oath or affirmation, and particularly describing the place to be searched, and the persons or things to be seized.

Amendment V

No person shall be held to answer for a capital, or otherwise infamous crime, unless on a presentment or indictment of a Grand Jury, except in cases arising in the land or naval forces, or in the Militia, when in actual service in time of War or public danger; nor shall any person be subject for the same offence to be twice put in jeopardy of life or limb; nor shall be compelled in any criminal case to be a witness against himself, nor be deprived of life, liberty, or property, without due process of law; nor shall private property be taken for public use,without just compensation.

Amendment VI

In all criminal prosecutions, the accused shall enjoy the right to a speedy and public trial, by an impartial jury of the State and district wherein the crime shall have been committed, which district shall have been previously ascertained by law, and to be informed of the nature and cause of the accusation; to be confronted with the witnesses against him; to have compulsory process for obtaining witnesses in his favor, and to have the Assistance of Counsel for his defence.

Amendment VII

In suits at common law, where the value in controversy shall exceed twenty dollars, the right of trial by jury shall be preserved, and no fact tried by a jury, shall be otherwise reexamined in any Court of the United States, than according to the rules of the common law.

Amendment VIII

Excessive bail shall not be required, nor excessive fines imposed, nor cruel and unusual punishments inflicted.

Amendment IX

The enumeration in the Constitution, of certain rights, shall not be construed to deny or disparage others retained by the people.

Amendment X

The powers not delegated to the United States by the Constitution, nor prohibited by it to the States, are reserved to the States respectively, or to the people.

The Declaration of Rights of the Stamp Act Congress
October 19, 1765

The "essential rights and liberties" listed by representatives at the Stamp Act Congress served as a precedent for the Bill of Rights that became part of the U.S. Constitution.

The members of this congress, sincerely devoted, with the warmest sentiments of affection and duty to His Majesty's person and government, inviolably attached to the present happy establishment of the Protestant succession, and with minds deeply impressed by a sense of the present and impending misfortunes of the British colonies on this continent; having considered as maturely as time would permit, the circumstances of said colonies, esteem it our indispensable duty to make the following declarations, of our humble opinions, respecting the most essential rights and liberties of the colonists, and of the grievances under which they labor, by reason of several late acts of Parliament.

1. That His Majesty's subjects in these colonies owe the same allegiance to the crown of Great Britain that is owing from his subjects born within the realm, and all due subordination to that august body, the Parliament of Great Britain.

2. That His Majesty's liege subjects in these colonies are entitled to all the inherent rights and privileges of his natural born subjects within the kingdom of Great Britain.

3. That it is inseparably essential to the freedom of a people, and the undoubted rights of Englishmen, that no taxes should be imposed on them, but with their own consent, given personally, or by their representatives.

4. That the people of these colonies are not, and from their local circumstances cannot be, represented in the House of Commons in Great Britain.

5. That the only representatives of the people of these colonies are persons chosen therein, by themselves; and that no taxes ever have been or can be constitutionally imposed on them but by their respective legislatures.

6. That all supplies to the crown, being free gifts of the people, it is unreasonable and inconsistent with the principles and spirit of the British constitution for the people of Great Britain to grant to His Majesty the property of the colonists.

7. That trial by jury is the inherent and invaluable right of every British subject in these colonies.

8. That the late act of Parliament entitled, "An act for granting and applying certain stamp duties, and other duties in the British colonies and plantations in America, etc.," by imposing taxes on the inhabitants of these colonies, and the said act, and several other acts, by extending the jurisdiction of the courts of admiralty beyond its ancient limits, have a manifest tendency to subvert the rights and liberties of the colonists.

9. That the duties imposed by several late acts of Parliament, from the peculiar circumstances of these colonies, will be extremely burthensome and grievous, and, from the scarcity of specie, the payment of them absolutely impracticable.

10. That as the profits of the trade of these colonies ultimately center in Great Britain, to pay for the manufactures which they are obliged to take from thence, they eventually contribute very largely to all supplies granted there to the crown.

11. That the restrictions imposed by several late acts of Parliament on the trade of these colonies will render them unable to purchase the manufactures of Great Britain.

12. That the increase, prosperity, and happiness of these colonies depend on the full and free enjoyment of their rights and liberties, and an intercourse, with Great Britain, mutually affectionate and advantageous.

13. That it is the right of the British subjects in these colonies to petition the king or either house of Parliament.

Lastly, that it is the indispensable duty of these colonies to the best of sovereigns, to the mother-country, and to themselves, to endeavor, by a loyal and dutiful address to His Majesty, and humble application to both houses of Parliament, to procure the repeal of the act for granting and applying certain stamp duties, of all clauses of any other acts of Parliament whereby the jurisdiction of the admiralty is extended as aforesaid, and of the other late acts for the restriction of the American commerce.

Source: The Constitution Society
http://www.constitution.org/bcp/dor-sac.htm

The Virginia Declaration of Rights
June 12, 1776

These rights, drafted by George Mason, were added to the Constitution of Virginia and became a model for the Bill of Rights in the U.S. Constitution.

I

That all men are by nature equally free and independent, and have certain inherent rights, of which, when they enter into a state of society, they cannot, by any compact, deprive or divest their posterity; namely, the enjoyment of life and liberty, with the means of acquiring and possessing property, and pursuing and obtaining happiness and safety.

II

That all power is vested in, and consequently derived from, the people; that magistrates are their trustees and servants, and at all times amenable to them.

III

That government is, or ought to be, instituted for the common benefit, protection, and security of the people, nation or community; of all the various modes and forms of government that is best, which is capable of producing the greatest degree of happiness and safety and is most effectually secured against the danger of maladministration; and that, whenever any government shall be found inadequate or contrary to these purposes, a majority of the community hath an indubitable, unalienable, and indefeasible right to reform, alter or abolish it, in such manner as shall be judged most conducive to the public weal.

IV

That no man, or set of men, are entitled to exclusive or separate emoluments or privileges from the community, but in consideration of public services; which, not being descendible, neither ought the offices of magistrate, legislator, or judge be hereditary.

V

That the legislative and executive powers of the state should be separate and distinct from the judicative; and, that the members of the two first may be restrained from oppression by feeling and participating the burthens of the people, they should, at fixed periods, be reduced to a private station, return into that body from which they were originally taken, and the vacancies be supplied by frequent, certain, and regular elections in which all, or any part of the former members, to be again eligible, or ineligible, as the laws shall direct.

VI

That elections of members to serve as representatives of the people in assembly ought to be free; and that all men, having sufficient evidence of permanent common interest with, and attachment to, the community have the right of suffrage and cannot be taxed or deprived of their property for public uses without their own consent or that of their representatives so elected, nor bound by any law to which they have not, in like manner, assented, for the public good.

VII

That all power of suspending laws, or the execution of laws, by any authority without consent of the representatives of the people is injurious to their rights and ought not to be exercised.

VIII

That in all capital or criminal prosecutions a man hath a right to demand the cause and nature of his accusation to be confronted with the accusers and witnesses, to call for evidence in his favor, and to a speedy trial by an impartial jury of his vicinage, without whose unanimous consent he cannot be found guilty, nor can he be compelled to give evidence against himself; that no man be deprived of his liberty except by the law of the land or the judgement of his peers.

IX

That excessive bail ought not to be required, nor excessive fines imposed; nor cruel and unusual punishments inflicted.

X

That general warrants, whereby any officer or messenger may be commanded to search suspected places without evidence of a fact committed, or to seize any person or persons not named, or whose offense is not particularly described and supported by evidence, are grievous and oppressive and ought not to be granted.

XI

That in controversies respecting property and in suits between man and man, the ancient trial by jury is preferable to any other and ought to be held sacred.

XII

That the freedom of the press is one of the greatest bulwarks of liberty and can never be restrained but by despotic governments.

XIII

That a well regulated militia, composed of the body of the people, trained to arms, is the proper, natural, and safe defense of a free state; that standing armies, in time of peace, should be avoided as dangerous to liberty; and that, in all cases, the military should be under strict subordination to, and be governed by, the civil power.

XIV

That the people have a right to uniform government; and therefore, that no government separate from, or independent of, the government of Virginia, ought to be erected or established within the limits thereof.

XV

That no free government, or the blessings of liberty, can be preserved to any people but by a firm adherence to justice, moderation, temperance, frugality, and virtue and by frequent recurrence to fundamental principles.

XVI

That religion, or the duty which we owe to our Creator and the manner of discharging it, can be directed by reason and conviction, not by force or violence; and therefore, all men are equally entitled to the free exercise of religion, according to the dictates of conscience; and that it is the mutual duty of all to practice Christian forbearance, love, and charity towards each other.

Source: The University of Oklahoma Law Center
http://www.law.ou.edu/hist/vadeclar.html

Miranda Rights

Miranda v. Arizona
384 U.S. 436 (1966)

Before a law enforcement officer may question you regarding the possible commission of a crime, he or she must read you your Miranda Rights. He or she must also make sure that you understand them.

Warning of Rights

1. You have the right to remain silent and refuse to answer questions. Do you understand?

2. Anything you do say may be used against you in a court of law. Do you understand?

3. You have the right to consult an attorney before speaking to the police and to have an attorney present during questioning now or in the future. Do you understand?

4. If you cannot afford an attorney, one will be appointed for you before any questioning if you wish. Do you understand?

5. If you decide to answer questions now without an attorney present you will still have the right to stop answering at any time until you talk to an attorney. Do you understand?

6. Knowing and understanding your rights as I have explained them to you, are you willing to answer my questions without an attorney present?

Source: The U.S. Constitution Online
http://www.usconstitution.net/miranda.html

Index